POLITICAL
BALDERDASH

Political Balderdash

iUniverse books may be ordered through booksellers or by contacting:

iUniverse
1663 Liberty Drive
Bloomington, IN 47403
www.iuniverse.com
1-800-Authors (1-800-288-4677)

ISBN: 978-1-4697-9584-3 (sc)
ISBN: 978-1-4697-9585-0 (ebk)

Library of Congress Control Number: 2012935070

Printed in the United States of America

iUniverse rev. date: 05/14/2012

POLITICAL
BALDERDASH

MICHAEL A. MAGGIANO

"An accumulation of the writings of
Political Science observer Michael A. Maggiano"

iUniverse, Inc.
Bloomington

23 PSALM

The LORD is my shepherd, I shall be in want.
He makes me lie down in green
Pastures.

He leads me beside quiet waters, he restores my soul.
He guides me in the paths of righteousness
For his name's sake.
Even though I walk through the valley of the shadow of death.
I will fear no evil, for you are with me;

Your rod and your staff, they comfort me.
You prepare a table before me in the presence of my enemies.
You anoint my head with oil; my cup overflows.
Surely goodness and love will follow me all the days of my life; and I will
dwell in the house of the Lord forever. Amen.

In Memory of my 3 Sons;
Michael III, Ronald & David
Bless Michael III, He is with the LORD . . .

ABOUT THE AUTHOR

At a young 85 last December the 27th 2011 Michael has been in music professionally since age 14, Michael and the Jolly Jesters Polka Band were doing Radio broadcasting one night weekly over WRRN in Warren, Ohio.

He has a broad industrial background in Quality systems and procedures writing in Engineering and Management with defense oriented precision types of products. He has a wealth of technical writing systems and procedures manuals for several companies on a consulting basis. In July of 2000, the Lord touched Michael via his Guarding Angel Saint Michael. Here is a short story on Elian Gonzales a Cuban boy strapped on an inner-tube in the Atlantic Ocean and hence forth picked up by two fishermen and taken to shore. This became my first piece of journalism. I kept up with the happenings for 6 months or more, until my head was spinning from all the so called government experts. It was like everyone knew the answers, but the balderdash continued with no solution forthcoming. I had it! So through my mind and fingers with the computer keyboard, out came the article. The editor, reviewed it and said it was great and well written, but too long, so I talked him into a Guest Column. A lady called me and said, "it was a masterpiece and flowed like poetry". Of course, I was the only Maggiano in the phone book. This was followed by 40 more articles in the opinion section of the Vero Beach Press Journal and the Ft. Pierce Tribune both in Florida.

Forward To Political Balderdash

This Book is devoted to an analysis of government systems with years of thought to improving, streamlining, restructuring, and tightened Total Quality Management through systemic alterations.

In congress as well as in the executive, I see no real use of TQM (Total Quality Management), or what little that might be used, has no teeth needed to cause real functioning of the systems which in my view are archaic to begin with. Lets relate the use of oversight to it's politically correct use by congress; view an update in Webster's New World Dictionary. The Dictionary in my research gives a meaning for "oversight" as a careless mistake or omission. Isn't it ironic that our troubles relative to the current Bailout, CEO's, golden parachutes and yes our "good old boy's and girl's" in our well intentioned congress, all have a hand in this monstrous undertaking. It falls on the back of the main street taxpayers for the good to all of the corruption, greed & collusion to the tune of trillions of dollars to the taxpayers. On top of all of that the Associated Press (2)shows $140 Billion Dollars for "Sweeteners to get the bill through congress". More corruptions! Where does hi-priced salaries of the congress' come into play. It seems to me that "congress is playing congressional roulette" with the electorate by holding the legal voters hostage. Is anything or everything fair game in today's government? Not the government I remember in my 85 years of life. There's greed, corruption, collusion and a total lack of real empathy for our fellow men, women and children in today's world and that's where humanity needs real reform! If it doesn't start NOW then we will continue to play to Lucifer's tune for the next 100 years or more!

I believe that our population and our government is too large and consequentially needs a complete restructuring for survival in a global society. The earth has a "World Bank"! How is it defined? What is it's earthly purpose? Does anybody know? I firmly believe that only a few people, those involved, know what it was created for and they're not letting it out! Where was it during and before the massive bailout in the financial wall street's needs for billions from taxpayer USA? I hesitate to include the many other companies that are part of this "Political Balderdash", the reason for the title of this book.

In THE EPILOGUE, I plan on answering some of the questions that will be reflected in some of the paragraphs that I have laid out. Further, it is my intent to relate major systems and government restructuring that will facilitate interaction between the States, and the Congress and the Executive Branch. It is important that the States retain their Sovereign Rights under the Federal Umbrella and make it unconstitutional for the Executive Branch to file a legal action against any state in the United States. There are better systemic ways to resolve problems that exist between the Feds and a State/s disagreement. Where is the Congress Hiding? Are they shirking their responsibilities? Congress bears the duty to solve the problem systemically without political tyranny and convulsions perpetrated as a result of legal action taken by the Feds against the State of Arizona.

America doesn't need a legal happy President that is ready to take legal action at the drop of a hat! That makes us look dictatorial to the rest of the World. This is a Great America!! Let us go back to the 140 Billion that was "sweeteners" for congress to get the 700 Billion stimulus done secretly at night behind closed doors. Was the aisle that separated the right from the left covered by smoked mirrors to maintain the lefts secrecy while they played congressional roulette in total disregard for the electorate of this Great United States of America. Then to make matters worse the same congressional roulette was played in secrecy to get the Obama care Health Bill through. It's time for the trillion dollar answer to the multi-trillion dollar question that was never asked?

Moreover, the bills should have been put to the electorate for a vote by the peoples government via a public vote to eliminate all the Balderdash in Congress! Why wasn't an investigation about "sweeteners' for congress to get the bill through. the electorate has a right to accountability by and through the Treasurer to account for the where, to whom, and why of every dollar of that 140 BILLION that should become known as—The "Golden Parachutes"—to get the Bills to fly, devoid of the electorate's unknown knowledge of the SECRECY perpetrated by the President's key players behind closed doors, known by the Executive Staff, obviously numbed down! Our government needs the inaction of a new Amendment that will create a Sunshine Law similar to Florida's congressional Law that devoid secrecy from the electorate and as well the congressional body.

ELLIOT NESS AND THE UNTOUCHABLES OF OLD

Why would I bring up the above title into today's world. I will explain as my article continues.

We the electorate who are familiar with what Elliot Ness was doing to clean up the corruption of gangster land which was running rampant in Chicago and today are hearing such published comments like "departed President Lincoln would turn over in his grave if he were cognizant of the political corruption going on in the Chi-town today". Well—in my view and opinion Elliot Ness would also turn over in his grave—Bless their souls as patriots of this great country.

As my 86th birthday nears, allow me to fast forward; Today's new untouchables have, in my opinion, emerged in the political arena by a form of gangsterism promulgated by a need for power, greed & corruption, identified with several legal terms in use today. There is much going on beneath the surface of politics that is not yet transparent but soon the unavoidable light will bring about transparency. Our political arena is in a shambles and until we have massive reforms in government in several major areas the necessary light will remain distant. The "do nothing Congress" has been functioning in a crisis management mode and those in the know, understand crises are not solved in that mode.

In retrospect, the Congress which should include the Executive, Senate and the House of Representatives, et al to be required to attend schooling as a side bar given by Instructors with strong knowledge in TQM (Total Quality Management) Systems and Procedures. In time it will be worth bags of Gold in all areas and especially streamlining and economics.

My 60 years in TQM gives me a solid base in writing, trouble shooting analysis, improving through changes and confirming the implemented actions from management, down through application use in the systems. The Peoples Government needs much tutoring in areas; kind of like teachers have to take courses and refresher courses to stay abreast of new systemic applications as they are confirmed for use. Remember, there are always better and more efficient ways to improve the Government! The government is no more or less than a huge corporate entity; and should be the goal of our congressional members to function in a TQM(total quality management) approach and make the necessary changes to assure a high level product comes off the assembly line ready for a consumer.

With my sixty years of all aspects of, and a practiced expert in systems and procedures in TQM, I have a right to know; it works in Congress and the political arena as well as the Executive Branch. It is not a good function in Crises Management; nothing is! It takes years to develop a proper intelligent mind set.

U.S. SOVEREIGNTY

As a Republic, we the legal citizens by birth and through attaining citizenship by proper means in accordance with the Constitution, The Declaration of Independence, and the many Amendments to the Constitution to date, thereby promulgated by Congress over time to the citizenry and legal electorate of the populace.

As a Republic; which we are in totality and as a Democratic Society; which "WE THE PEOPLE" are striving toward; with the many obstacles that create much pain; and are exacerbated by congress during the many years is my opinion. We dare not exclude the Executive Branch and the elite of the elites known as Congress. The elites are so far reaching, it's important that Wall Street and Corporate America not be left out of the equation which includes obstacles of pain. That sort of an equation would make Einstein's Equation of Relativity become dwarfed by our governments attempt at the huge bill on health care by way of the two branches of our government having dyslexia with such a bill Pres. Obama and Manager Reid lead to hopeful fruition. I haven't read the book that would be too big for me to even carry! My transparent observation is that even a Philly Lawyer would have a real chore reading and correlating this massive manuscript.

What happened to KISS (keep it simple stupid)? In my opinion, there is a lot of intellect in D.C. with a lack of Transparency that has been transformed to the political power secretly!

The Trillion Dollar Question is: Why is a large part of the electorate upset and thumbs down on the health bill? They can't all be wrong! Is this monster of a bill too big to fail? A roll of the dice tells me that the Health Bill has a far better chance of doing just that! In my excess of 40 years in Quality Assurance from the bottom up through technician, analyst, engineering, management, writing and teaching. My boss and mentor PHD, Dr. Hugh Rogers considered me the best\\humble Quality Practitioner he had ever worked with at Valencia Community College in Orlando, Florida.

My judgmental opinion is built on a simple approach that the high secrecy within the closed doors were clouded by a series of smoked mirrors, defusing the realities of the so called results. Perhaps, that was the reasoning for Ms. Pelosi making the comment that the huge book would be read after it was approved and properly signed. REALLY!

When did we the electorate let the horse out of the stables prior to fully checking the cart to make sure the cart meets the requirements; that an instability might cause a long and arduous trip to passengers without potential delays and repairs; by the wayside at a cost of billions to the corporate entity of the American citizenship! I think an ounce of prevention is worth millions of pounds of cure! Stay out of crisis management and also Political Balderdash!!

THREE WEEKS OF THE REALITIES OF ILLEGAL IMMIGRATION! APRIL 13, 2006

YES AMERICA—We have watched an invasion of our borders, our cities, our streets, our highways, from the south-west-east-north. It bothers me and also millions of other citizens who have had their normal lives nearly brought to a screeching halt. Moreover this was being done while the politicos were on their spring break. However, it didn't stop the children of illegal parents from leaving school to enjoy joining the demonstrations that were tying up the aforementioned rights of way through out our very populous large cities.

The silent majority and the baby boomers of this nation that are not illegal, should be asking, in mass the following questions: did the perpetrators/leaders that concocted this national event get legal permits? Did school-skipping children get written parental permission to leave the school grounds? Do they have any idea of the cost to the legal taxpaying public? Do they know or believe in the "Golden Rule"? If you answered "yes", you failed the test. I could go on, but enough food for thought! Oh, one other question : What is happening to our country's sovereignty? Sorry people, but we are fast becoming a cesspool of illegal immigrants. It wasn't—when our parents had to come from foreign lands and meet stringent laws to enter this country. Multiple standards today allow almost any body to cross our borders.

This is a sad commentary, however it is very real. So—is the high and mighty senate going to reverse the house passed immigration law and placate the illegal immigrants through some form of amnesty, no matter how they sweeten the words. Violating two or more laws of the land, that the majority have to abide by, demands punishment for those that disregard such laws.

Michael A. Maggiano

Mini-Preface

This article was published as a Guest Column in the Vero Beach, Florida Press Journal Newspaper in July, 2000. It relates to Elian, the little Cuban boy that was picked up by two fishermen in the ocean outside of Florida. After six or more months of frustrated nonsense, I decided it was time for writing my first article, and so I did and so it was published as a Guest Column in my name with a photo of me from years past. Florida has a law that indicates that if an individual, not a citizen, lost in the ocean, makes it to shore by his feet touching shore on his own, the person has a right to plead citizenship. That was not so in Elian's case. Of course he was a small boy. Read and enjoy the article.

GUEST COLUMN

Elian saga highlights greed

The Elian saga depicted by the many news reporters and journalists was just another travesty in our country, the country that most of us citizens love and care about. However, there are questions that should have been asked. The questions not having been asked, consequently were not answered.

First, let us explore the initial period when Elian, tied to the floating inner tube in the Atlantic Ocean, was picked up by the "fisherman" and brought safely to land. The INS law is clear that because Elian did not by his own efforts set foot on land, as an alien he was not entitled any form of asylum and should be held by INS for return to Cuba to his father.

This then poses questions. Did the fisherman bypass the INS and take Elian directly to someone that the fisherman knew as distant relatives? If so, by what authority? Was the INS contacted? Did the INS find out about the incident after Elian was in the control of the distant relatives? If so, why didn't the INS go and retrieve the child and make him a "ward of the state" until Elian could be returned to his father in Cuba?

I believe this approach to the incident was the proper way for the INS to have handled the situation. This I have discussed with some people from the very beginning. It would have eliminated the months of haranguing, unlawful legal chess games, illegal harboring of an alien child and the least, by far, expense to the taxpayer. But then that would have eliminated the need for a "surrogate mom."

The truth about these questions, I believe, is known. but then the questions were never addressed. I've followed this saga very closely and never heard journalists or any other news media pose these questions. Therefore, no answers were given by Janet Reno or the INS. I have my own answers to these questions and, given past performances by our authorities, I believe that they deemed it was easier just to leave things lay rather than take constructive action before it was too late. None of this should have gone beyond the first two days after Elian's rescue.

Then we have politicians and journalists (some being lawyers) making statements that the issue should be referred to the family court. How preposterous! We have an alien child, not a U.S. citizen, being harbored by distant relatives, a father in Cuba and the issue should be solved in the family court. When did the family court start including aliens on their dockets? What makes the whole episode even more ludicrous is that we have "Little Havana," including the officials in Miami, functioning as a separate entity without regard for the laws in the United States and even defying such laws. Still no action taken.

GUEST COLUMN CONTINUED

[Michael Maggiano, a Vero Beach resident is employed by Indian river Community College. He was an adjunct professor in industrial management technology at Valencia Community College.]

Finally, Janet Reno had to take the actions necessary to bring the standoff to closure in the best interests of the young lad and his father. I have disagreed with Miss Reno on many other past actions or the lack thereof. I feel in this case she was left without any real alternatives, thanks to the distant relatives and "Little Havana" for taking matters into their own hands like the many occurrences in the past by many other people in our country. If they choose to do such things, I say fine, go back to their homelands and do them but not in this country that millions have fought and died for. As an upper-class senior and a WWII veteran, I have a right to know.

There is one more question: Who is paying the bill for the millions that have been spent by accumulated costs of time by lawyers, INS, the judicial system, Congress, housing for Elian's real family, the numerous trips, court costs, etc.? If I were sitting in the White House, I would have an answer. Aside from that, *you know who!*

Was this all done in the best interests of Elian? I don't think so. I think this was all done with dollar signs toward the future. There has been talk of a book and what follows a book? Need I ask? I never saw a time when Elian's surrogate mom's appearance wasn't television camera ready. Notoriety as a financial staple is running rampant in our country, as well as in the world today. It all equates to greed! Regard for morals, life, liberty and the pursuit of happiness have taken a back seat to materialism. Destructive indicators are becoming more and more prevalent.

It's time for all true Americans to be looking at what kind of legacy we are leaving to our future generations. Attitudes among people need to be reformed like some of our government systems surely need reformed. There is lack of good and proper respect for one another, as well as a lack of right and just examples in the human chain from the very top to the bottom link in that chain. I believe this is all tantamount to the continuity of life. Think about it America!

DESTROY EVIL AT ITS HEAD
(FT PIERCE TRIBUNE NOV. 8. 2001)

Now that President Bush, his Cabinet and the military advisors have started positive action against the terrorists, their camps and their infrastructure in Afghanistan, as well as a World War II veteran, I'm totally in agreement. He was sufficiently patient to allow time for getting all the military conditions in order and ready to go. The military force must incur and demand all the pain possible on the evildoers of Osama bin Laden and his Taliban tentacles that stretch out like those of a monstrous octopus. In order to destroy such a monster, you must incapacitate it at the head. This analogy I got from my dearly departed father: "All fish rot from the head down." Like poisonous snakes, if you decapitate one, the body nerve reflexes will continue the striking motion until the nerves die from lack of blood and oxygen.

If you do this to Osama and the Taliban, the tentacles will soon cease to exist. However, they must be made to feel pain they will never want to feel again, with or without Allah's approval, for their deeds through the lying promises of bin Laden and his evildoer commanders and terrorists supporters. I don't take highly to bin Laden calling Americans and our president infidels. It is said that it takes an infidel to think they recognize one. This evil one that poses as a cleric is a devil in a "cleric's" image. He and his followers must be removed from the face of the earth in order for the real peace of God and the peace on Earth's civilization to return. It is my belief that President Bush and his advisors clearly understand these principles. they are to be commended by all united Americans for their exemplary actions and concerns for the public's well-being both here and abroad. In late 1989, I entered a contest to earmark the decade of the '90s. I entered "the implosive decade of the nineties." Many implosive things happened in that decade—in our justice areas, in our executive branch, in our Congress, in the voting arena, and severe destruction of properties both inside and outside of our country. The '90s was just the tip of the iceberg. We are seeing a continuum of the previous decades on Sept. 11, 2001. In my view, the world is in the period of the anti-Christ and Osama bin Laden—the Anti-Christ—and the al-Qaida the disciples of the devil/

evildoer, bin Laden. He has made himself to appear like a Christ but his actions and words are those of the devil.

In conjunction with Attorney General Ashcroft, the FBI, the CIA and the newly created Homeland Security, it is crucial to rout out all the evildoers in our great country. This needs to include hoodlums that are responsible for the rioting that has hurt people and destroyed property of other law-abiding citizens. it needs to stop for the good of the country. We are a nation of laws for the well-being of all citizens. I thank these agencies for the great job they are doing under severe, adverse circumstances.

In conclusion, God bless our government and the unified, peace-loving people of the world. Finally, bless the U.S.A. and be with us in times of sufferance and help keep us strong.

Michael A. Maggiano
Vero Beach

THE TALI BAN TENTACLES

GLOBAL TERRORISM

Michael A. Maggiano

Mini Preface for 'IRAQACY' Leads to Democracy

The writer of the article created the word 'IRAQACY' to define the Iraq's newly created government in their forth coming country's regulations. It is my desire to include the word into the Dictionary as permanently used word to reflect Iraq's newly formed government of the People of Iraq

NOVEMBER 18, 2002

U.S. WILL PREVAIL OVER SADDAM

It is time to review the historical facts, impediments and answers as to what we know about what we are dealing with in the Iraq situation.

So let's first go to the historical facts:

> ➤ From the time of the war on Iraq to free Kuwait from Iraq tyranny and invasion, we have given Saddam Hussein far too much time to further his capabilities of weapons of mass destruction.
>
> ➤ The Iraqi madman is crafty like a fox vying for the hen house. He allowed the inspection of his country, through the U.N. resolution, for chemical, biological and nuclear weapons of mass destruction. Saddam found every conceivable way to thwart the terms of the resolution to the point of its cessation.
>
> ➤ Why didn't we take Saddam out after freeing Kuwait? It ties in with our political arena modus operandi. To me, it equates to "we won the war but delayed the peace." Now we have to do it again.
>
> ➤ Now let's go into the impediments:
>
> ➤ There is Russia sitting on the fence. It seems to me that many of the countries that accept our assistance in many cases are blind to the despicable threats upon the world by a madman, one who will not rest until he achieves the results necessary to become a force to be reckoned with.
>
> ➤ Our Congress wants transparency from the executive branch. They want to put their two cents worth of fodder into the question. Kind of like they did in the Vietnam War, where it was fought via Congress, not by generals in the field of battle. We just can't learn lessons from the past. Congress considers themselves the voice of the people. Did they consult the people when twice they gave themselves an overnight increase to a figure of $150,000 annual as public servants? These are just some of the more glaring impediments. There are numerous answers as to our dealings with Iraq. The one that hits the hardest is the cat and mouse game, the

chicken game or the transparent chess game. We in America have allowed the cat to play the game of terror, deception, lies and what else you can bring to mind for over 10 years and with the blessing of the United Nations. These are monstrous impediments to achieving world peace. As you might understand it, yes, we are the mouse in this game or at checkmate if playing transparent chess. We won't talk about "chicken."

➤ Secondly, in the transparency game, what happened to the various classes of security in the government—top secret, secret and confidential security clearances? They are not being promulgated to the fullest as necessary in a time of war against terrorism. This was absolutely necessary in World War II, even in defense plants and the lines dare not be crossed. Yet the Congress wants transparency. Ask Sen. McCain about security clearances. He knows the drill. I also know the drill. I had to go through it in a defense plant. Our modern, liberal congressmen and women coupled with the ACLU need to get a real life. These are impediments because terrorists have big ears, fat wallets and they need to be decimated. I can find a whole lot more need for eliminating transparency chess games. But food for thought is sufficient for now.

I would like to express one serious caveat that I have not heard expressed so far. Though I am fairly certain it it in the minds of our defense team that I hold in high regard. My big concern is the protection of our military men and women from harm's way. How can we do that? We have the capabilities with our known highly technological defense and offense equipment as recently demonstrated. We must use whatever it takes to fully neutralize Saddam's weapons of mass destruction before sending in ground troops. It should be absolutely clear to we Americans that Saddam would not bat an eyelash in the use of weapons of mass destruction on our troops as he did on the Kurds. This is one thought that does need transparency. Weapons inspection in Iraq is not a solution to the problems, just another delay tactic. Wake up, U.S.A.

We shall prevail. God bless all Americans.

Michael A. Maggiano
World War II veteran
Vero Beach

Mini Preface

This Mini Preface is to highlight the strong reflections that show loose congress trying to function in a helter—skelter crises mode, which never works within a framework where the word oversight due to oversights resulted in things missed that made the problem more difficult to corral and correct the problem. Congress needs to refrain from the use of the word oversight. It's incorrect use will only cause more grief in Congress.

PUT 'AMERICAN' BEFORE ETHNICITY

Politically correct?

Reference the Fort Pierce *Tribune* article dated Thursday, Sept. 13, titled "Area Muslims condemn attacks," by staff writer Jason Geary.

This letter questions the fifth paragraph, first sentence, which reads "Throughout South Florida, American Muslims reacted with horror to Tuesday's attack." I question the political correctness as perceived by today's journalism and examples in the last eight years or more by the political arena. To be politically correct American Muslims should have read "Muslim-Americans." In every instance in long years past all ethnic groups with the exception of the American Indian, the ethnic ancestry had taken precedent over being American. This decries Americanism.

I can't get into your head so it befuddles me as to whether it was an oversight or intentional. I'll presume it was an oversight.

I would like to tell my story:

Incidentally, I will soon be 86 years old and have seen much. My parents came through Ellis Island in the beginning 1900s. That was when immigration was very tight with stringent requirements. A person had to have $50 on your person and sign papers to be educated to learn to read, write, and speak English (to 8th-grade level), albeit with an accent. They were Italian.

There were seven children and I was the youngest, in a very poor family. My parents spoke to us in English albeit it was somewhat broken. I've always given them credit for showing Americanism. They would speak to each other in Italian, but to us and in public they spoke English to the best of their ability. In time they became better at it.

The main message in this letter, especially in light of the terrorist attack on the Trade Center, is that we all become dedicated Americans, except for illegal immigrants. We are all American citizens once citizen status is achieved by birthright or through application granting citizenship.

This and numerous other so-called politically correct approaches need to be altered. I say this in the best interest of America. We must meld into one nation under God. I would like to see the word American brought to the forefront over ethnicity through legislation in Congress to emphasize Americanism. For example, American-African, American-Haitian, American-Italian, American-German, American-Muslim, etc., etc., etc.

Mr. Geary, I am in agreement with your well-written article. I commend you on good thoughts and contents. I would like to petition you and all other Americans to write our congressional representatives and request that they formulate a simple bill to accomplish this objective. I will send copies of this to politicians from the Cabinet on down. I believe we have been in the wrong mode for years.

Michael A. Maggiano
Vero Beach

Ten Commandments for terrorists

Having pondered this over and over in what's left of my 77-year-old brain, I feel a strong desire to discuss the tentacles of terrorism.

A simplistic version of "The Ten Commandments":

1. I, the Lord, am your God. You shall not have other gods besides me.
2. You shall not take the name of the Lord, your God, in vain.
3. Remember to keep holy the Lord's day.
4. Honor your father and mother.
5. You shall not kill.
6. You shall not commit adultery.
7. You shall not steal.
8. You shall not bear false witness against your neighbor.
9. You shall not covet your neighbor's wife.
10. You not covet anything that belongs to your neighbor.

My analogous version of "The Ten Commandments" reflects how the international terrorists' commandments, if they had them, might read.

I would like to make it absolutely clear that the following has in no way been directed at the good practicing Islamic people, either here or abroad. But it exemplifies my view of the terrorists and their inimical values and teachings of the devil (their Allah):

1. I, the Devil, am your Allah. You shall not have other Allah's besides me.
2. You shall take the name of your Allah in vain.
3. Remember to keep holy the day of the devil.
4. Do not honor your father and mother, only yourselves.
5. You shall kill all infidels to enter the Devil's paradise.
6. You shall commit adultery as you choose.
7. You shall steal and maim at will.
8. You shall bear false witness against all infidels.
9. You shall covet your neighbor's wife.
10. You shall covet anything that belongs to the infidels.

Praise to good humanity and God bless all infidels, worldwide.

Michael A. Maggiano
Vero Beach

Stop tearing down administration

Yes, America, the double-digit number of presidential left-wing aspirins (They give me a headache. Whoops, you get the message) should stay in their armchairs. They would do the American public more good there.

Many citizens, including myself, can be capable of punditry. However, presidential aspirants in excess of a dozen only reflects an inherent pattern in the left-wing Democratic approach to a formulated "best defense is a good offense." Your stupidity doesn't understand that this premise is only good in football and sports, most assuredly not good in politics—far too transparent to the majority ruling/voting public. Intellect and common sense prevails, not egomania, greed, sole party gratification, self-notoriety, to name a few idiosyncrasies that belie all the Democratic aspirants.

The constant tearing down of the present administration should make it absolutely clear that unless the aspirants have walked in the shoes of the current administration, the aspirants should put some duct tape over their mouths or bite their tongues real hard until it hurts them where it does them the most good. They all border on conspiracy toward the government of the United States of America.

My remaining words are "if that's the best we have" for the Democratic Party, heaven help us in this great America that most of us love. That includes you, too, Hillary and "Slick Willie" Clinton.

Michael A. Maggiano
Vero Beach

THE ENSUING BATTLE OVER GUANTANAMO BAY MARCH 31ST. 2003

After watching the Jay Leno show and not being sleepy, I was cruising the channels and stopped on C-Span. As luck would have it, former Vice President Dick Cheney was about to come on with his speech in rebuttal of our new (Heinz-57) President Barrack H. Obama's approach to the dilemma in the Guantanamo stockade.

I digress momentarily about the words in parentheses above. Congress uses earmarks in its functions and I have in my opinion earmarked Mr. Obama as a Heinz-57 president. Why?

I, like many Americans, am unclear about the who, what, where, etc., of his adult life. Is his pastor of 20 years a patriot? "Without doubt, a need for clarity and where there is smoke there is usually fire."

If Mr. Obama were put through top-secret security, like many in World War II, would he pass? We have a right to know; it is our government—of, by and for the people. We, the people, have no desire to be sold down the river to terrorists.

Terrorism needs eliminated by whatever means we undertake, but most certainly not through our court system. Terrorists have no rights to our legal system and we best not allow that. Treat them as the devil's disciples, which they are, and to prevent any other 9/11s.

I agree with the totality of Mr. Cheney's speech of May 22. I would like to see American citizens create strong congressional pressures to impeach the president, Nancy Pelosi, Harry Reid and any others who side with the liberal approach of Mr. President's legalese with the terrorists.

Stay out of Guantanamo for the good of America.

Michael A. Maggiano
Vero Beach

SPECULATION ON WHITE HOUSE MARCH 31, 2003

A look into 2008 deals with the presidential election. My view deals with my perception of the main players on the United States stage. Some of the past of the players. The present players. The tactics of the future players. No, I do not have a crystal ball, but foresight and I seem to have some of that which gives me the ability to at least write about it. I see on one side of the political spectrum the former president and the current senator of New York. These domiciles in my view were pre-planning for 2008. Now, why would I think that?

Well, it sort of goes like this:

Let me start with former President William Clinton. Many including myself like to refer to him as "Slick Willie." He had charm, good looks, he could speak among the best, and he was a saxophone player, as I am. Now just a little touch of laughter. "I used to say that the president best do a good job or if he didn't he would surely give saxophone players a bad name." However, as time went on and things came out about him and as more time went on it became clear that the liberal Democratic Party was wrapped around his liberal finger.

Now, at this point, I would like to stress that I am not a rabid political party person. As a matter of fact, I decry the party system. Why? Because my belief is that the party is not good for a republic system of democracy. The constant bickering across the aisle is sometimes more that I care to tolerate. It causes many undue delays. Also, it has ceased to be an effective bipartisan instrument of a people's government.

Back to our former president. Admittedly, I am not well informed about his youth. However, I opine him in the White House as an egocentric spoiled adult. One who pouted about having to leave the presidency. further, in my view, he is still pouting. He found a home there. He did all the cajoling he could during the mess he found himself in with the young female intern. He wasn't man enough to step down for even the good of removing the tarnish he brought to the highest office in the land. More recently, both Mr. Clinton and Mr. Carter are violating the ethics of being former presidents in order to try to overcome the stigma that has been brought about by these party losses during the recent election. They have lost sight of the fact that you can catch more bees with honey and the old rule that if you can't speak decently of someone you shouldn't speak at all, especially of the current president. This reinforces my disdain for party politics.

Think about the scheming that took place in Clinton's election, when many thousands were given voting rights prior to the second election. No checks of any kind were made prior to this event. Think about the fact that they all should have been checked out in order to cull out undesirables, criminals or ties to outside criminals. This wasn't important. What was important to the scheming DNC candidates was the vote increase at any cost. However, most of the real thinking public understood this, but failed to think about the side effects on the general public. What percentage of undesirables, criminal and worse did this self centered approach allow to be walking among we the people?

Why did Slick Willie after all his shenanigans in the White House energize his first lady into the Senate? Think about the Clintons and their over whelming desire for the White House and all the scheming they did while there. Well, I see them up to their old tricks. The Clintons want to make more history. I see them attempting to put Hillary in the White House in 2008. That way Slick Willie will overcome his pouting. Secondly, that will have achieved a first. A former president who by all odds should have been removed from the White House while in office is able, through scheming, to return to the White House. Heaven help this country should it happen.

Finally, during the mess with Mr. Clinton's shenanigans, his defiance to be removed from office with the help of his liberal senators, it was Hillary Clinton who made the accusation that it was all a big conspiracy against the president. Again, in my foresighted view, that show of unity by the Clintons was a smokescreen toward solidification down the road to the year 2008.

Does America want the Clintons in the White House for another four years or more and more? The thought repulses me, but I am only one of perhaps multitudes. It's your decision, America.

Michael A. Maggiano
Vero Beach

SNAKE CHARMER, SNAKE MUST GO

SATURDAY, JULY 6, 2002

The Snake in the Sand and the Snake Charmer.

Conditions in the Middle East brought to mind the titled article. It prompted the writer to create a mental image.

The Palestinian Chairman Arafat's head garb, from my first sighting in the news, has reminded me of a king cobra in human flesh. Having felt that, coupled with my continued attention to the news, I decided to write this article.

My mental image further sees Iraq's Saddam Hussein as playing the role of the snake charmer with the golden instrument that he uses to charm the snake to do his biding.

Now, before the readers think I am a nut, read on. Arafat and Hussein are the players in my visual depiction.

There is no doubt in my mind that Arafat is being mesmerized by the golden tones of Hussein's snake charming melodies. It's a Middle East approach to a puppet with strings on the Palestine Stage of Terrorism, via suicide bombers/murders. It seems absolutely clear that the inability of Arafat to control such actions is influenced by some outside driving force. Consequently, where there is a Snake in the Sand there must be a Charmer somewhere nearby. The teachings of money for martyrdom at any age is deplorable to humanity and abusive to children. Those responsible for such teachings must be reformed or removed from society.

Why is Saddam the Snake Charmer? What is in it for him? It is apparent to many, if not most of the world, that the Charmer is paying the families of the suicide bombers/murders for their despicable deeds of suicide to kill innocent bystanders. These are mentally sick people.

Saddam the Charmer will use any lying tunes to help retain his waning power in the area.

Cost to a madman is not an issue. With a mentality of total disregard for human life, except his own and those that protect him, nothing else matters. Wake up, America. The Snake and the Charmer must both go for the good of humanity.

Michael A. Maggiano
Vero Beach

The Snake and the Charmer

Gibson's vision, Democrats' words

I treated myself to a showing of Mel Gibson's "Passion of the Christ." Though I enjoyed it immensely, my mind turned to all the talk coming from the liberal armchair quarterbacks for the past months.

During the verbal antics that led up to everyone chanting "Crucify Him, crucify Him," I thought of the rabid liberal crowds behind the Democratic aspirins (they give me a headache). In their own rabidity they might as well have said of President Bush: "Crucify Him."

Their untruths were as shallow as the minds of the speakers and the cajoling done to create a frenzy in the crowd was akin to the movie. However, the outcome will be different; a crucifixion will not take place. Bush will, in my opinion, prevail.

The voting public must beware of wolves in sheep's clothing. Learn all the facts about the political aspirants as a guide to casting your votes.

Michael A. Maggiano
Vero Beach

DEMOCRATIC HOPEFULS
GIVE HIM HEADACHE

The double-digit number of presidential left-wing aspirins (they give me a headache, whoops, you get the message) should stay in their armchairs. They would do the American public more good there.

Many citizens, including myself, are capable of punditry. However, presidential aspirants in excess of a dozen only reflect an inherent pattern in the democratic approach to a formulated "best defense is a good offense."

Your stupidity doesn't understand that this premise is only good in football and other sports. In politics, it's far too transparent to the voting public. Intellect and common sense prevail, not egomania, greed and self-notoriety, to name a few idiosyncrasies that belie all the Democratic contenders.

The constant tearing down of the present administration should make it absolutely clear that unless the double-digit aspirants have walked in the shoes of the current administration, they should put duct tape over their mouths or bite their tongues real hard until it hurts. Their rhetoric borders on sedition toward the government of this United States of America.

If this is the best we have from the Democratic Party, heaven help us in this great country that most of us love. That includes you, too, Hillary and "Slick Willie" Clinton.

Michael A. Maggiano
Vero Beach

SOCIAL SECURITY

Wake up, seniors; Congress has slept in

The Social Security cost-of-living increase may be eliminated for the next two years. Why? Only the elites in the Senate, the House and the administration have the answers.

As a World War II veteran and a senior, I would suggest that all citizens raise the roofs in D.C. through all the aforementioned elites, by whatever means are at their disposal, with a strong message that we are entitled to life, liberty and the pursuit of civil happiness within our constitutional rights.

Through a socialistic approach, seniors are being put out to pasture like cattle. Our needs as humans will not be a part of the equation in a socialistic society. That is just a start!

How about the "notch babies" born between 1917 and 1926—an error period in the annals Social Security. The notch fiasco has been bantered in and out of Congress for years, only to be tabled when presented for action.

Do I need to go further and accuse Congress and the administration oversight (in the real meaning of the word)? Look oversight up in the dictionary—Nos. 1 and 2 of three meanings.

Congress bears much complicity due to a lax approach that led to financial deterioration. This has been exacerbated by a lack of total quality management and poor systemic procedures. Nothing's changed.

Michael A. Maggiano
Vero Beach

MADAME SPEAKER'S (DICTATORIAL) HOUSE SHUTDOWN

Three cheers for the recent rebellions that took place in the Representatives, the American Citizen's House in our Congress of the USA. In my analysis, Ms. Pelosi, solely by her actions, perpetrated a despicable, disgraceful act of authority without discussion or even a hand vote by the people's elected Members of the House. "Here's your hat, what's your hurry"! Madame Speaker needs a lesson in tact and diplomacy for use on the House members, the American people and her own benefit.

If Ms. Pelosi's five week vacation was of dire importance in nature, she had options available to her if she truly cared about the public and the crucial economical straits that America is in at this time. Her choice could have been to put the majority leader in charge until her return. Obviously the thought was not part of her mind set, or perhaps that would detract from her empowerment of females, which seems uppermost in her mind today. Is that in her job description? Not likely, in my analysis. What if Ms. Pelosi became ill and had to be hospitalized for a time, I don't wish that on her, but what if? Would the Peoples House shut down! Think about it!

My opinion is that Madame Speaker wouldn't make a pimple on a good Speaker. As far as empowerment of women—they have been empowered more than enough since WWII. Enough is enough!

The other thing that comes to mind is—that presumed presidential aspirant Barack Hussein Obama is quietly backpedaling the self made crisis by Ms. Pelosi.

The American Voters should write or email their representatives and ask that Ms. Speaker be fired on the spot. In most industries that would happen, due to failure affecting crucial schedules!

SEVERE QUESTIONS IN WASHINGTON D.C.

Let's start this article back in 2008 when the Associated Press published the article that was about the $700 Billion Bailout of the U.S. financial system. The next item in the article was $140 billion for sweeteners to get the bill through Congress. This raises many questions? First, under what congressional traceable procedure did this dispersion occur? Second, who was the issuing department and by what controlling systemic paperwork? Third, who signed for that vast amount of billions of dollars and the responsibility for recording the signatures of the recipients and the monetary amount received; without controls, could be swept under a large carpet! Why sweeteners, to begin with? Was an investigation started? I don't recall any relative news of any investigation. If, I am in error, some one enlighten me, for the record!

Fast forward to current events. Now we have a new or newer problem facing congress. We have a new company on the horizon. the company's name is Solyndra. Their item is Solar Panels. I just became aware of it through the news. The questions; who authorized the $535 million for the company's start-up? Was this a presidential sole action? Was Congress involved in any interim action and/or questioning of the CEO's. Was any form of congressional approval or was this all about the President's new job plan or his twelve member committee action. Never the less the news is out that this new company has filed for bankruptcy. This must be some of the President's Green Job creating program. But in my view, it's likely to cost the taxpayer's BILLIONS. Will it never STOP!!

PONZI SCHEMES are in the air, America!

U.S. PAIN POSTULATES TERRORISTS PAIN

Now that President Bush, his cabinet and the military advisors have started positive action against the Terrorists, their camps and their infrastructure in Afghanistan, as a WWII Vet I'm in total agreement. He was sufficiently patient to allow time for getting all the military conditions in order and ready to go. The military force must incur and demand all the pain possible on the evil doers of Osama bin Laden and his Taliban tentacles that stretch out like those of a monstrous octopus. In order to destroy such a monster, you must incapacitate it at the head. This analogy I got from my dearly departed father, "All fish rot from the head down". Like poisonous snakes, if you decapitate one, the body nerve reflexes will continue the striking motion until the nerves die from lack of blood and oxygen. Don't try this at home! I saw this with my own eyes. If you do this to Osama and the Taliban the tentacles will soon cease to exist. However, they must be made to feel pain they will never want to feel again, with or without Allah's approval, for their deeds through the lying promises of bin Laden and his evil doer commanders and terrorist supporters.

I don't take lightly to bin Laden calling Americans and our President—Infidels. It is said that it takes an infidel to think that they recognize one. This evil one that poses as a cleric is a devil in a 'clerics' image. He and his followers must be removed from the face of the earth in order for the real peace of God and the peace of Earth's civilization to return. It is my belief that President Bush and his advisors clearly understand these principles. They are to be commended by all United Americans for their exemplary actions and concerns for the public's well being both here and abroad.

In late 1989, I entered a contest to earmark the decade of the 90's. I entered "the implosive decade of the nineties". Many implosive things happened in that decade; in our justice areas, in our executive branch, in our congress, in the voting arena, and severe destruction of properties both inside and outside of our country which affected the U.S.A. I believe I should have won except for myopic judges who could not see beyond their nose. Many of our citizens are also myopic as reflected during the Florida voting fiasco.

The 90s was just the tip of the iceberg. We are seeing a continuum of the previous decade as of September 11, 2001. In my view, the world is in the period of the Anti-Christ, and Osama bin Laden—the Anti-Christ and the al Qaeda the disciples of the devil/evil doer bin Laden. He has made himself to appear like a Christ but his actions and words are those of the Devil!

In conjunction with Attorney General Ashcroft, the F.B.I., the C.I.A. and the newly created Homeland Security it is crucial to rout out all the evil doers in our great country. This needs to include hoodlums that are responsible for the rioting that has hurt people and destroyed property of other law abiding citizens. It needs to stop for the good of the country. We are a nation of laws for the well being of all citizens. I thank these agencies for the great job they are doing under severe adverse circumstances.

In conclusion, God Bless our Government and the unified peace loving people of the world. Finally, bless the U.S.A. and be with us in our times of sufferance and help keep us strong.

Michael A. Maggiano
Vero Beach, Florida

CONFLAGRATION SEARS
FLORIDA VOTER ARENA

Yes Florida, for a month now a great and destructive fire has been raging throughout this state. This fire was not started with some source of inflammable material that some fire bug might use. Instead, it was started with vocal incendiaries, by the Democratic National Committee (DNC). these flames were fanned by a flock of parrots/lawyers that came down from the DNC in Chicago and vocally fanned the flames. They were joined by a multitude of other parrots from the Gore camp to help fan the flames until the partisan fire grew into a great and destructive force.

This vocal fire has gotten completely out of hand, so much so that it started spreading to various other parts of Florida and to other states. It enjoined partisan voters into legal action to further fan the vocal flames. Consequently, the fire became bipartisan in nature in order to try to keep the fire from reaching out of control proportions. Now the court system has been brought into the foray, to help neutralize the out of control situation. It seemed to have little anti-inflammatory effect.

The vocal parrots had been out in force gathering affidavits on the butterfly ballot, signed by voters in the three county area to direct the vocal flames at over turning the election to the loser. Seems to me this is just another way of fanning the flames of vocal destruction, clearly, without regard to the Republic and charring the office of the Presidency in the eyes of the world.

After two machine counts and invalid hand counts, the vocal fires raged on. What's it all about Alfie? Is the burning desire to be President at all costs to Florida and the voters who voted correctly or incorrectly, justification for devious approaches to winning. Multitudes of correct voters think not!

Vero Beach, Florida
Michael A. Maggiano

PALM BEACH AREA VOTERS CRY WOLF!

The reason for this article is to express my concerns and the realities of the Palm Beach Area fiasco and the perpetrators behind it. First, let me interject my political position. I vote my conscience independently of the contents of the ballot. The primary registration that requires you to specify a party affiliation, I believe, is invalid and unconstitutional. My plan in the voting booth on election Tuesday was to write in John McCain for President, but not having properly prepared myself to do so, I had to make a choice of my mind. Now that I have gotten that off my chest, allow me to go on to the subject matter at hand.

The Palm Beach voters that cried wolf after they left the voting booth and tried to leave the booth door open so that they could "cry foul" through legal action, after being prodded by the DNC Hierarchy, need to grow up!! Sorry folks, but everyone only gets one chance in the voting booth. Once you put that ballot in the ballot box, if you messed up, you have only to look in a mirror and tell the person in the mirror "I messed up "and live with the errors of your way. I might add that the DNC from Chicago who swooped down on the Palm Beach area like vultures looking for a feast have credentials that are less than "lily white" and prone to win at any cost to the detriment of the voting public and the Republic as it stands in awe. I make note of the fact that during the election day, I commented "that if the election was close with G.W. Bush winning" the DNC would cry "foul". It doesn't take a rocket science scholar to recognize childish behavior. Especially after V.P. Gore had conceded late on election day to Gov. Bush and then retracted his concession. Is that what we want as our leader? One who makes claims but speaks out of the other side of his mouth in retrospect.

It is very clear that the problem lies with the electorate and is exacerbated by the local DNC and their Chicago leaders and I use the word leaders loosely. This is not some devilish concocted "right wing conspiracy" as we have heard from Hillary in the past in defense of her husband. To add insult to injury we find the DNC asked for a recount, then a second recount both of which favored Gov. Bush by similar margins. But that wasn't good enough for the Gore camp, so coupled with their local allies they took it upon themselves to start a hand count. this is America folks! Why weren't the opposition, who had the edge on count, consulted? This is called getting the jump in warfare and sports. The creators of corruption and multiple standards during the last eight years, now want to create a new multiple standard in the voting arena. "Continue the campaign and the voting effort until the desired end results are achieved". That's my statement!

Believe me Fellow Americans, at age 75 and having dealt with people errors as a Quality Practitioner, Quality Engineer, Quality Manager, Systems and Procedure Writer and Analyst as well as Technical Teaching since 1950, I speak volumes and with practiced authority.

Now let us go into my valid rebuttals to what has been going on and why actions by the Gore Camp are invalid and if they are allowed to continue they will become bogus. Further they are creating division and deviousness in the Republic and Florida. Let's look at this as a process which is what it it. The voting booth is the main operating equipment. The so called butterfly ballot or other type ballot is the product. The flaps with the candidates names on them are accessories and the tool is the hand punch that is used by the operator (the person doing the voting). It is all very straight forward and very simplistic. The problem is in the operator (voter). If there is a sight problem or other kinds of vision problems; if there are physical handicap problems, such as arm or hand strength; the equipment, accessories, punch tool are sound and checked before they are positioned for use. If the operator is visually or physically impaired they should ask for help, however in many cases voters won't ask for help and if they punch the wrong hole and then realize their error and punch the right hole that becomes a reject during the automatic counting. Also if the voter doesn't push the punch pin to where it bottoms out, or they may think they have but haven't, then there could be a variety of conditions that could cause rejects during the automatic counting. Voters, especially, are very secretive about voting. It's hard for me to understand why. But these are inherencies in humans, but never the less and invalid reason for the debacle that is being perpetrated by supposedly affluent and intelligent people. My knowledge encompasses the design and manufacture of these machines, tools and accessories as well many other types of equipment of very complex and highly precision in nature, their assembly processes, testing and uses.

Secondly, the hand counting is invalid because the counting is done in a selective manner. In accordance with all sampling procedures of which Military Standard 105E the latest Revision from which all sampling procedures are derived from. (Page 4 Par.3.20 is very clear that selectivity is not randomly and states "the units of the sample being selected at RANDOM without regard to their quality"). So all the people in this façade are only using their mouths and not their god given brain and thereby bastardizing statistical processing and sampling standards that are clear and nationally used. A standard bell curve is what we have now with Gore on one side of the norm centerline and Bush on the other side of that line. What the DNC and their talking parrots/attorneys are trying to do is use validly rejected product which is not reworkable in order to askew the sigma limits of a normal bell curve with rejected product in favor of Gore. This is fraud in my book and in accordance with standard practices within the industries. If this happened at NASA we would have lost a lot of lives trying to get to the moon.

I agree with everything that is being said about the voting public except that human error is the part of the equation that must be considered in making a final and accurate decision in the voting arena and the voter mistakes need to be recognized as an unavoidable inherency. Further that the voting public that made the errors need to accept their errors and go on. In Quality Assurance circles there is an idiom that says "you can do your best to make a process fool proof but you can't make it idiot proof". That's no reflection on the voting public, that's human nature.

Michael A. Maggiano
Vero Beach, Fl. 32962

Michael A. Maggiano

I wrote this-my very first poem-to the present President G.W. Bush for his July 6th birthday. At 80 years old, I felt compelled-I know not why-to try to reach all of the citizens of our country that respect, humility, and grace should be accorded to all Presidents-past, present and future. as a self-made non-poetic writer, I have written and had published numerous Articles in local newspapers. I am presently working on two books and hope being published in poetry.com will help in the book publications via exposure through your Library of Poetry.

I am very grateful!

AN ODE TO OUR PRESIDENT

2000-2008

Let us not forget our flag that flies in majestic splendor or the words "IN GOD WE TRUST",

And let us be reminded that the greatness of our country is a must!

As Americans from all earthly lives we must remember the burning embers of the past that pervade the present,

And cries aloud for humankinds sake that any Presidents task is not "a piece of cake".

Whoa be unto those who lack humility, from heavens grace, lest they look in a mirror and see their face,

And ask their self, "am I in disgrace-is that really me", lest they might say in a humble way,

"God Bless you Mr. President and God Bless The U. S. of A"!

Michael Anthony Maggiano, II
June 2006

SENIOR AMERICANS—WAKE-UP!!!

I have bantered this around verbally for a couple of weeks and now it's time to put it on hard copy. According to the latest out of Washington the Social Security Cola (cost of living increase) is to be eliminated for the next two years. Why, you ask? Only the Elites in the Senate, the H of R, and the Administration have the answers. As a WWII veteran and a Senior, I will express my opinions. However, first I would suggest that all citizens raise the roofs in D.C. thru all the fore-mentioned Elites, by whatever means at their disposal with a strong message that we are entitled to life, liberty, and the pursuit of civil happiness within our constitutional rights!

In my view, through a socialistic approach in today's world, I see the early stages of we Senior's being put to pasture like a herd of Cattle, so our needs as humans will not be a part of the equation in a socialistic society. That is just a start!! How about the notch period that senior's were born in (1917 to 1926) an error period in the annals of social security. The Notch fiasco has been bandered in an out of congress for nearly 10 years only to have it tabled when presented for action by congress. Do I need to go further and accuse congress and the administration of oversight (in the real meaning of the word). Look oversight up in the dictionary, 1 and 2 of 3 meanings.

Whatever it's worth in my opinion congress bears much complicity due to oversights in many areas in 2008 of a financial nature lax approach that led to financial deterioration due to a lack of TQM (total quality management) and poor systemic procedures and no controls via lax oversight with little or no strong management. Nothing's changed!

THE SOLAR FORCES AND OUR ENVIRONMENT

We here on earth need to start thinking SUN! Why would I make such a statement? Also, why at this time would NASA send up a Delta 2 rocket to carry a STEREO satellite into orbit to measure the sun and solar wind in 3-D? Is this a first? Or has NASA done this in the past? The present Delta 2 was launched on Aug. 20, 2006. It would be interesting to note the past history of NASA's data relative to prior satellite launches and their purposes and findings data wise. It is not to my recollection from the past, but then I am not involved 24/7.

My reason for writing is because for too many years I have been preaching the Sun and it's relative effects on our earth and the environment. Until we can gather certain data, over time, the speculation becomes the blind leading the blind. The monstrous variables on the sun and the solar winds they create and the electro-static energy of a positive and negative nature created by humongous solar arcs become unthinkable to the majority of humankind. Can NASA measure these data? Perhaps! This is just the "tip of the iceberg". The earth is a live planet in our solar system undergoing unfathomable changes from early years AD. So many variables today—unplanned growth—huge metropolises being created and built without thought of diminishing effects-

Let's bring the Earth's finite variations into the picture. How about wobble and the finite effect on the earth's north/south axis as it relates to the sun? How about the finite variables in the earth's path around the sun and as it rotates on its axis.? What data has been achieved over time that can be applied? Can science effectively and accurately measure such data? How is the weight displacement of the huge cities on the earth affecting it's wobble, rotation and orbital path around the sun? Food for thought, the earth is here but has undergone many changes since 1000 AD.

You might say weight displacement has no effect on changes of the earths orbit, rotation, wobble and the angle of the north/south pole axis. I disagree with that hypothesis. I haven't included earthquakes, tsunamis, volcano's, earth's plates shifting and removal of huge oil, gas and mineral resources for civilizations use or the weight loss due to the many vast forest fires throughout the world that result in weight changes. Then there are the huge cities on this planet with vast weights centered in vast areas; Singapore, Los Angeles, San Francisco, Chicago, New York City to name just a few of the weight factors in trillions of Tons. In my theory, we have insufficient data to even consider a formula to equate the Earth variables as they relate to orbital, rotation, axis and wobble, not to bring into play the power of the Sun and the solar winds that we, to date, have little or no data/base to put to mathematical tests of theories This is all just the tip of the so-called iceberg. Global Warming: the Sun, Solar Winds and the Earth!!!

However, lets take two simple scientific analogies as real food for thought and very miniscule as related to the sun and it's planet earth. First, think auto tire assembled to a wheel. Then think small variations in thickness of the rubber due to heating and cooling of the rubber during the molten process of the raw materials. Now add lead weights to compensate for these variations to bring about a balance at hi-speed rotation on a balance machine. An inverse hypothesis—if the weights are removed or improperly placed on the wheel, the out of balance will reoccur. Second, think a fast spinning top like kids like to spin and yes adult kids, too. Now, blow into the side of the rotating top and increase the air velocity, blow harder. The top should tilt slightly.

ARIZONA HAS STATES RIGHTS

With respect to all the political nonsense that is being postulated by Hillary Clinton and the Obama care cabinet, they are all wet in their approach to the immigration law to protect Arizona's electorate and curtail the massive illegal invasion south of the border.

My opinion leads me to believe the Secretary of State is all wet. She is preaching to the Hispanic choir and she may very well throw out the baby in the very muddy bath water. I can't believe that the federal government is considering a law suit against Arizona. That's an intolerable thought. The states sovereign rights need to come into play at this point. Further, all the other Southern border states, including California, Texas and Florida should join the foray.

Since I lived in Arizona for over 25 years since 1955, I have heard and seen much with the ongoing Illegal Invasion. I would cite an experience in the late 50s. As new to Phoenix, my family got into a casual conversation with a Hispanic lady and in bringing Arizona into the talk, the lady said "Arizona doesn't belong to the United States, it belongs to Mexico". She said it with Mexicali gusto!

Do we want to bring another Spanish-American altercation into view from the past? the Executive branch of our government is irresponsible to the needs of the states illegal immigration invasions and Congress as well. Hillary Clinton indicates the law in question invites racial profiling, but in reality her words will instead incite more illegal's to cross the borders. There is a big difference between profiling and the need for controlling the invasion. Conversely, you are hurting the Arizona electorate. In my view, Hillary, you owe them an apology, in writing! (1)

You might have used the words "SAFE PROFILING" for the good actions of both parties. As our Secretary of State, you blew it Hillary. What's right is right and wrong has Human interests at stake on both sides of the border. Further, you fanned the flames of hysteria on the illegal's who don't want to know the difference. Their only purpose is money through greed at the expense of Taxpayer USA! They're using every rope from within and without; through risking their lives and our Border Guards safety by ruthless Drug Lords or any way possible. Where are the Mexico Federalize! On a Daily siesta, Maybe? Former President Fox and his successor have made no attempts to secure their Borders! They leave their control up to the "GOOD OLE USA", "WE ALLOW IT"! So it Appears! We need another TEDDY ROOSEVELT!!!

Finally, "does America need a President who at the drop of a HAT, will have his Atty. General file a legal suit against Arizona's Governor! An unheard of such an action in the annals of US history. What was his real purpose? Where instead, the problem should have been turned over to Congress for a resolution, in fact one was really necessary. How much is the President's action going to cost the taxpayer by the time the action ends up in the US Supreme Court for a final decision. My acronym M-B-T (million-billions-trillions), comes into play here. This is a form of economizing!! Can you believe that?

GROUND ZERO AND SHARIA LAWS

I am about to venture on an unknown thought followed by a scary opinion on the subject title of this writing. At this point I will bring to light my much used, "this is a very sad-bad commentary to bring onto the Great American People".

It's time for food for thought. Mexico's Presidents Calderon and Fox came here and bad mouthed our country, as did recently in the news media—the Imam Fesal Abdul Rauf executive director of the Gorboda Initiative? Sly foxes from wherever on earth, are past masters of deception.

Two articles published by the Associated Press in the Press Journal dated respectively on the 19th of Aug. and Sept. 5th, 2010, look on the internet, they would suggest we have a good ability to read between the lines, in order to get into our minds some of the ideals of terrorists minds. The articles are about Islam and U.S. Muslims. who fear trouble about 9/1, and rightfully they should, due to the disasters perpetrated by their peers on 9/11.

Now their hierarchy want to bring about pluralism among the religious beliefs in our country through the 15 story Mosque as a cultural center or whatever they, (down the road) decide to call it. Their secrecy is almost on a parallel with our congress during the Health-Care debacle.

Remember American citizens, untruthful Sly Foxes abound everywhere on earth!

There is absolutely no room for either pluralism or duplicity where our laws are concerned. Their Sharia Laws cannot apply! Their people must abide by the laws of the USA!

The ACLU needs to stay out of any thoughts of pluralism or duplicity of intermingling any SHARIA LAWS with our Constitutional Laws and the finality of our Supreme Court!

AMERICA—IT'S TIME TO WAKE UP AND STOP THIS
BALDERDASH in it's tracks-NOW!!!

Pay heed America: The best way to undermine the USA is by intermingling
any foreign legal system with our American Legal System. It's imperative
that our Congress create an Amendment to the Constitution and further
that the Executive Branch cannot file any legal action against any US
State in our Union. Any thoughts of such an action, must be by memo
in writing to Congress for action and resolution of the problem. Legal
actions by the Executive's can cost the taxpayer's millions or billions of
dollars. I'm certain the Arizona game of congressional roulette is holding
hostage the electorate. Where is the economizing going while the Fed's
and the many states are involved in a legal cat and mouse comedy. Who
is running the countries legal business? Where is Congress? Siesta's take
place in Mexico not in our Congress!(2)

Our Secretary Of State, Hillary Clinton, while she was in Arizona, made a
statement that was published in our Press Journal newspaper that Arizona
was treading on "racial profiling" by the law created by Arizona's Governor.
Hillary's use of the word "racial" should instead have been the word "safe"
profiling, unless she was preaching to the Hispanic Choir(caucus), created
by Ms. Pelosi and sworn in by "her majesty" Speaker of the House. For
shame on me for my reference "her majesty"!

In my opinion, we should omit (through legislative amendment) all
caucus'; they are nothing more than(PAGs political action groups.
What happened to the American Congress and Executive Branch of our
Government. They are being watered down by ethnicities from outside of
our borders. The allowable of which is a consternation to the American Way
of True American Ideals. Further, over time, America will start to loose it's
sovereign strength as The United States of America!!! We must get REAL
and dispense with all variations of POLITICAL BALDERDASH!!!

Otherwise, intelligentsia will continue down the slippery slope coated with
manure. Think about it in the coming elections down that Slippery Slope!!
Remember the INCUMBENTS that should be replaced. Especially by all
you Seniors who went for TWO YEARS WITHOUT A COLA, while

congress got hefty hefty increases, where is the justice, America—and the inflation is CLIMBING at a good rate!!

So much "Balderdash" is coming out of Washington, it's in unbelievable secrecy that the slippery manure coated slopes will facilitate the barrels of corn fodder on their way into the chasms below. Heaven help the USA! The solutions are there, their just hidden in smokes and mirrors.

The blame game continues. The other party did it! The former President is responsible even though the power changed well over three long years ago. Change was promised! Where did the indicated change get lost? In the Political Balderdash, maybe! Wake up America!! Institute My Reconfiguration Plan and save our American Electorate, Now! The Federal Umbrella has a tear or crack and needs repaired by knowledgeable means!

My Reconfiguration Plan is not instantaneous, however once instituted, with all of the pandemonium going on through the country, it's timely and can be a permanent solution. The Reconfigure plan will be detailed in the last section of the EPILOGUE. It's not new to me, it's been in my head for ten or more years. Read it intently and try to visualize it. It's an expansion of our first Colony with a streamlined approach to the growth of America and the retention of the importance of our Statehood under a Defective Federal Umbrella!

My sixty years of varied background in from small to large diversified corporations, gives me a strong edge in the Total Quality Management through their requirement of systems and procedures. These can apply to any applications including governments, financial institutions, industrial ventures, large and small countries, and any space ventures in our universe! We need to start with our Planet-America as the greatest Country on this Planet.

"It's a MAD,MAD,MAD,MAD WORLD"

In the early sixties, the above movie came out. I remember it well. I got a DVD copy from the public library. At the age of 82 years I enjoyed a review. It was a comedy spoof with a large fabulous Hollywood Cast from that era. The movie stars to name just a few included: Jimmy Durante, Milton Berle, Spencer Tracy, Sid Caesar, Buddy Hackett, Ethyl Merman and many other great stars. It's a classic and I highly recommend it for viewing by the general public throughout the US of A. It exemplifies the corruption, greed, power hungry, money, thievery, drugs and a liberal immoral society that is at least a thousand times worse today and I haven't addressed murders.

Why would I suggest viewing the above movie?

* Primarily, it reflects a strong need for personal introspect into humankind with strong needs for improvement with fervor toward a more peaceful national community for our children, adults, and the coming generations in the 21st century.
* Secondly, we need to do it by right actions, deeds and empathy toward those that are crying out for help. Find a copy of the ten commandments, memorize them and seriously do your best to adjust your life accordingly. Peace and solitude will prevail in time.
* Finally, if there are any thoughts or hopes for a globalization of society, and WE THE PEOPLE of the United States of America is expected to be the MODEL for the global entity, then we the citizens of this great US of A best start setting good strong examples today, tomorrow and the rest of our God given natural lives.

THINK ABOUT IT AMERICA!

Whatever else you do in your life, as you read this article, please see and enjoy the movie!

May 20, 2008

EPILOGUE TO POLITICAL BALDERDASH

This lengthy chapter is devoted to an analysis of government systems with years of thought to improving, streamlining, restructuring, and tighter Total Quality Management through systemic altercations and Amendments to the Constitution.

In congress as well as in the executive, I see no real use of TQM (total quality management), or what little that might be used, has no teeth needed to cause real functioning of the systems which in my view are archaic to begin with. Lets relate the use of oversight to it's politically correct use by congress thru an update in Webster's New World Dictionary. The Dictionary in my possession gives a meaning for "oversight" as a careless mistake or omission. Isn't it ironic that our troubles relative to the current Bailout, CEO's, golden parachutes and yes our "good old boy's and girl's" in our well intentioned congress all have a hand in this monstrous undertaking that falls on the back of the main street taxpayers for the good to all of the corruption, greed & collusion to the tune of trillions of dollars to the taxpayers. On top of all of that the Associated Press shows $140 Billions Dollars for "sweeteners to get the bill through congress". More corruption! Where does hi-priced salaries of the congress come into play. It seems to me that "congress is playing congressional roulette" with the electorate by holding the legal voters hostage. Is anything or everything fair game in today's government? Not the government I remember in my 85 years of life. There's greed, corruption, collusion and a total lack of real empathy for our fellow men, women and children in today's world and that's where humanity needs real reform! If it doesn't start NOW then we will continue to play to Lucifer's tune for the next 100 years or more!

I believe that our population and our government is too large and consequentially needs a complete restructuring for survival in a global society. The earth has a "World Bank"! How is it defined? What is it's earthly purpose? Does anybody know? I firmly believe that only a few people, those involved, know what it was created for and they're not letting it out! Where was it during and before the massive bailout in the financial wall street's needs for billions from taxpayer USA? I hesitate to include the many other companies that are part of this "Political Balderdash", the reason for the title of this book.

In this epilogue, I plan on answering some of the questions that will be reflected in some of the paragraphs that I have laid out. Further, it is my intent to relate some major systems and government restructuring that will facilitate functioning between the States and the Congress and the Executive Branch. It is important that the States retain their Sovereign Rights under the Federal Umbrella and make it unconstitutional for the Executive Branch to file a legal action against any state in the United States. There are systemic ways to resolve problems that exist between the Fed's and a State/s disagreement. Where is the Congress Hiding? Are they shirking their responsibilities? Congress bears the duty to solve the problem systemically without political tyranny and convulsions perpetrated as a result of legal action taken by the Fed's against the State of Arizona.

America doesn't need a legal happy President that is ready to take legal action at the drop of a hat makes us look dictatorial to the rest of the World. This is a Great America!!

A brief of my vision of the US of A verses the UN of A. In my view, the influx of legal and illegal immigrants are totally out of a normal invasive, uncontrolled influx across our borders and Ports is surely having a strong watering down of a true American ratio which incites me into a need of save America solution. Inconsequently, we are fast becoming a United Nations of America! In time if we Americans fail to do some serious reversal of these actions, it will soon be too late! Is that what we want for America!! All the signs seem to indicate the slippery slope is becoming more heavily coated with manure and the chasm is directly ahead! Whoa America! reverse engines!

This last phase of this Epilogue deals with my Reconfiguration program, which ties into my Sixty years of systemic background; technical writing, teaching, analyzing, inclusion into the particular system, debugging the results and writing the changes for the final approval.

US of A Reconfiguration

I will go into the overhaul configuration in a simple approach, followed by a structured Total Quality Congressional and Executive detailed systemic sequence. There will be important caveats noted. It might be interesting to note that I have toiled on this for ten to fifteen years or more. I have some sixty years in TQM(total quality management) in a variety of industrial companies; in highly precision production and assemblies in Aircraft high speed rotating turbine engines and diversified manufacturing and assemblies. Also developed and taught a variety of specialized courses in industrial precision inspection. Just an overview of my sixty years of background, including solid rocket motors.

My approach is to strengthen the sovereignty of the statehood by going back in time to the thirteen colony period under the British King rule. America was subjected to tyranny and convulsions. Which we needed to get away from and the politico's of today are on a reverse to that era, due to a total lack of strong leadership in the executive branch and in congress as well; a lack of their existing awareness. Secretary of State Clinton inferred that Arizona was treading on "Racial Profiling" but as US Secretary of State, she should have used a better choice of words like "Safe Profiling" to keep Arizona safe from drugs and illegal entry resulting in a form of political tyranny and convulsions, as well! This is also true in the southern Texas-Mexican borders!!

In the decades past, both Texas and California had thoughts of secession, (along with other Southern States), from the Federal Union (1860-1861). That never happened, historically, to my recollection.

My reconfiguration will be noted as recon for ease of simplification. In systemic sequence we must realize that from the initial 13 colonies/states, America has grown in statehood to four quadrants; we the now US of A, has 50 states which includes Alaska and Hawaii. It's necessary to introduce 2 more states. We do 2 State Referendum's; Divide Texas into East and West and California into North and South. Now we have 52 States devisable by 13 gives our statehood 4 equal colonial quadrants(States). The Northeast original colony; Southeast colony includes Florida and East Texas, followed by the South west colony which includes West Texas, Hawaii and South California, the Northwest colony includes Alaska and North California. Each Quadrant becomes one of the whole US of A. This would require 2 new governor's, one in Texas and one in California.

The next step in the systemic process is the creation of the position of a well qualified Executive Technical Vice President of each Colonial Quadrant. The responsibility will be to work with the Quadrant Governor's to streamline their states to improve jobs, their economy, bring jobs back into the quadrants and find ways to expand the needs for more workforce through a strong shot in the quadrants arms and coordinate with the Feds when necessary.

The recon into Quadrants may require a National referendum. This is all built around retaining the States Sovereign Rights per the Constitution. With 13 states in each of the Colonial Quadrants and an Executive Technical Vice President in each of the four Colonial Quadrants will create a New United States of America and reduce the power of the federal Branch to the President's Oversight responsibility to the needs and assistance of the Statehood Quadrants and the diplomatic approaches with other Countries and our allies as well as our two Protectorate Nations that at some time in the future may become more than just Protectorate Nations.

There is a tear or a crack in the Federal Umbrella, which needs repaired by a Broad Scope of varied intellect. The intellect of a neighborhood organizer lacks the depth totally necessary to repair the crack or tear in the Federal Umbrella and should retire back to neighborhood undertakings. If Elliot Ness was aware of the disjointed picture in our government, he is likely to turn over in his grave, like many others have done in the last three years.

Lets revert back to the Recon. Some other changes need to take place. One is the words of the members of congress and the executive branches, at their swearing in. "We will become politically neutered, during our term/s of our position held", in the interest of the well being of the electorate, in general, as well as our constituents! The main aisle will no longer be a divider of the right or the left. The entire congress must become bi-partisan to get things done for 'we the people' of the US of A! Also, the members will take TQM familiarity courses to streamline procedures in the use of the Oversight practices to prevent Oversights. It's necessary to have valid discussions not blatant balderdash!

The Quadrants can be in competition to improve all things necessary to make the Reconfiguration process viably to sustain the US of A for another one hundred years for the well being of the future generations and the return of the America ahead to the GOOD TIMES once again and reduce the placating of the rest of the world to LIMITS!

Mini Preface

The Quadrants of the respective States
within it's particular Zone(N.E., etc.) each
have the Thirteen States in that Zone.

N.E. Quadrant

Maine
New Hampshire
New York
Pennsylvania
Massachusetts
New Jersey
Maryland
Ohio
Rhode Island
Michigan
Wisconsin
Connecticut
Delaware

N.W. Quadrant

Washington
Oregon
N. California
Nevada
Montana
Wyoming
Utah
Colorado
Alaska
N. Dakota
S. Dakota
Nebraska
Idaho

S.W. Quadrant

S. California
Arizona
New Mexico
W. Texas
Kansas
Oklahoma
Missouri
Minnesota
Iowa
Arkansas
Kentucky
Hawaii
Nebraska

S.E. Quadrant

Florida
Georgia
S. Carolina
N. Carolina
Louisiana
Mississippi
Tennessee
Alabama
E. Texas
W. Virginia
Virginia
Indiana
Illinois

PALM BEACH AREA VOTERS CRY WOLF!

The reason for this article is to express my concerns and the realities of the Palm Beach Area fiasco and the perpetrators behind it First, let me interject my political position. I vote my conscience independently of the contents of the ballot. The primary registration that requires yon to specify a party affiliation, I believe, is invalid and unconstitutional. My plan in the voting booth on election Tuesday was to write in John McCain for President. But not having properly prepared myself to do so, I had to make a choice of my mind. Now that I have gotten that off of my chest, allow me to go on to the subject matter at hand.

The Palm Beach voters that cried wolf after they left the voting booth and tried to leave the booth door open so that they could "cry foul" through legal action, after being prodded by the DNC Hierarchy, need to grow up!! Sorry folks, but everyone only gets one chance in the voting booth. Once you put that ballot in the ballot box, if you messed up, yon have only to look in a mirror and tell the person in the mirror "I messed up" and live with the errors of your way. I might add that the DNC from Chicago who swooped down on the Palm Beach area like vultures looking for a feast have credentials that are less than "lily white" and prone to win at any cost to the detriment of the voting public and the Republic as it stands in awe. I make note of the fact that during the election day, I commented "'that if the election was close with G.W. Bush winning" the DNC would cry "foul". It doesn't take a rocket science scholar to recognize childish behavior. Especially after V.P. Gore had conceded late on election day to Gov. Bush and then retracted his concession. Is that what we want as our leader? One who makes claims but speaks out of the other side of his mouth in retrospect.

It is very clear that the problem lies with the electorate and is exacerbated by the local DNC and their Chicago leaders and I use the word leaders loosely. This is not some devilish concocted "right wing conspiracy" as we have heard from Hillary in the past in defense of her husband. To add insult to injury we find the DNC asked for a recount, then a second recount both of which favored Gov. Bush by similar margins. But that wasn't good enough for the Gore camp, so coupled with their local allies they took it upon themselves to start a hand count. This is America folks! Why weren't the opposition, who had the edge on count, consulted? This is called getting the jump in warfare and sports. The creators of corruption and multiple standards during the last eight years, now want to create a new multiple standard in the voting arena. "Continue the campaign and the voting effort until the desired end results are achieved". That's my statement!

Believe me Fellow Americans, at age 86 and having dealt with people errors as a Quality Practitioner, Quality Engineer, Quality Manager, Systems and Procedure Writer and Analyst as well as Technical Teaching since 1950, I speak volumes and with practiced authority.

Now let us go into my valid rebuttals to what has been going on and why actions by the Gore Camp are invalid and if they are allowed to continue they will become bogus. Further they are creating division and deviousness in the Republic and Florida. Let's look at this as a process which is what it is. The voting booth is the main operating equipment. The so called butterfly ballot or other type ballot is the product.

The flaps with the candidates' names on them are accessories and the tool is the hand punch that is used by the operator (the person doing the voting). It is all very straight forward and very simplistic. The problem is in the operator (voter). If there is a sight problem or other kinds of vision problems; if there are physical handicap problems, such as arm or hand strength; the equipment, accessories, punch tool are sound and checked before they are positioned for use. If the operator is visually or physically impaired they should ask for help, however in many cases voters won't ask for help and if they punch the wrong hole and then realize their error and punch the right hole that becomes a reject during the automatic counting. Also if the voter doesn't push the punch pin to where it bottoms out, or they may think they have but haven't, then there could be a variety of conditions that could cause rejects during the automatic counting. Voters, especially, are very secretive about voting. It's hard for me to understand why. But these are inherencies in humans, but never the less an invalid reason for the debacle that is being perpetrated by supposedly affluent and intelligent people.

A BORDER CONTROL SOLUTION APRIL 9, 2006

This is a solution that I have given intense thought to for four or more years. Now I feel it is the time to engender my laborious thoughts, and a systemized process. Let me be clear that I bear no animosities toward any ethnicities, secularities, or of colors that want to become citizens of our great country. I do, however, decry the millions of illegal aliens that are here and those that avoid the many legal ports of entry. They pay big money to smugglers that help them reach our borders.

Secondly, they work for employers that benefit from their illegality. Two wrongs, in most cases, don't make them right. We have laws against unlawful entry and trespassing, whether it be via state, federal or privately owned land. These violations are compounded by hiring illegal workers. The money they earn mostly goes back to their country. We must alter their mental thinking by a form of punishment that makes the outlook of their illegal ends less desirable. They will work for room and board. This would apply to the millions of illegal people that are already in this country. If we intend to solve border control, we in America must be bullish about it. Amnesty for illegal entries won't solve the problem! It will only make it worse!

Finally, the solution in short:

* Tighter border and port control.
* Set up in each border state in the south (including Florida) and on the north borders a compound similar to the Civilian Conservation Camps of times past (I believe there are still some available).
* The border patrol in conjunction with state police will take any caught illegal entries to the camp to be processed and confined for a year or more. They will be on controlled work detail where needed.
* Their pay with the exception of a small petty cash will go from the employer to a federal border control treasury department. This will accomplish many important things.

1) keep the money from going out of the country.
2) Use the money to self perpetuate the border control system.
3) Most importantly to discourage illegal entry and encourage entry through legal ports of entry.
4) Through being punished for violating the laws of illegal entry and trespassing the perpetrators will be checked out for any other criminal history, drug related background or terrorist activities.
5) Be required to learn to read and write the American language.
6) Be documented and sign the necessary forms when they are picked up. Their smugglers will be put thru the same requirements and will also be guilty of smuggling.
7) This will alleviate the employers of hiring non citizens as workers.
8) This will send a clear message to other countries leaders that America will not tolerate illegal entry across U.S. borders from other countries and should induce their leaders to inform their citizens of the penalties they will face for not entering the U.S. by legal procedures.

Make no mistake that the millions of illegal people in the United States should be subject to these same conditions as they are in violation of the same laws of being illegal and trespassing no matter how long they have been here. There should be only one standard not multiple standards for the laws of the U.S. of America. Our country needs to revert back to the very stringent requirements when Ellis Island was the only way for immigrants to get into the U.S. I know that today our multiple standards has created an immigration cesspool that is fast destroying our citizens rights as a sovereign nation. Thanks to our former President Johnson's "New World Order"!

FEDERAL ACTION AGAINST ARIZONA?

As a former Arizonan (ref. *PI* opinion article—Mrs. Clinton-dated wed. May 19,2010). I have been in disagreement with her and upset at the precedent that the executive branch is setting from a legalese standpoint. I'm not an Atty., but common sense tells me that Arizona can coalesce with other States that agree with Arizona's new law, get together with Arizona and file a class-action counter-suit against the Executive's and let it go to the US Supreme Court for a decision. I totally disagree with the thought that Arizona is inviting racial profiling. Arizona and other south border states are looking down that same road of invasion from without and convulsions within. Look in the Declaration.

Is Hillary Clinton as I stated in my article, preaching to the drug lord's and the Latino Choir and the politico atmosphere for votes in the coming elections? You and the Execs. are dead wrong for playing political tyranny and congressional roulette at the expense of the electorate who are entitled to life, liberty and the pursuit of happiness under God and man and women. Think about it Mrs. Clinton. You are a citizen of America, not Mexico! Incidental to Mexico, when the new president from Mexico spoke here, he should have been told tactfully to go back and control his people away from our borders- by whatever means his Federalize' have to take. Hopefully he needs to go back with his tail between his legs. Like President Fox when he was here during President Bush was in control. I had published a similar article at that time and indicated that President Fox Should keep his foxes and coyotes' out of the American Henhouse.

That goes double for our President and Mexico's President. Is America getting too soft?

This last page of the Reconfiguration Plan is imperative that Congress review it and discuss the future implementation in order to bring about the necessary systemic alterations to undue the damage that will continue unless Congress takes the actions that will stop all, the Balderdash the Feds are up to and think Electorates needs to unify and to become the decision makers. That's expected of them and refuse to be cajoled by an Executive Branch that has done nothing except to slide the electorate in the can that's on it's way down the slippery slope coated with more manure. Think about it Congress! There are better ways to avoid the coming Chasm!

My 60 years of Systemic and Total Quality Management background make it so!!